Brazil

TARA WALTERS

Children's Press®
An Imprint of Scholastic Inc.
New York Toronto London Auckland Sydney
Mexico City New Delhi Hong Kong
Danbury, Connecticut

Content Consultant

Hannah H. Covert
Executive Director
Center for Latin American Studies
University of Florida
Gainesville, Florida

Library of Congress Cataloging-in-Publication Data

Walters, Tara, 1973-
  Brazil / by Tara Walters.
        p. cm. -- (A true book)
  Includes index.
      ISBN-13: 978-0-531-16851-6 (lib. bdg.)
              978-0-531-20725-3 (pbk.)
      ISBN-10: 0-531-16851-4 (lib. bdg.)
              0-531-20725-0 (pbk.)

  1. Brazil--Juvenile literature. I. Title. II. Series.

  F2508.5.W35 2007
  981--dc22   2007036022

Produced by Weldon Owen Education Inc.

12 11 10 9 8 7 6 5 4 3 2   08   10 11 12 13 14 15/0

Find the Truth!

Everything you are about to read is true *except* for one of the sentences on this page.

Which one is **TRUE**?

T or F It is a lucky sign if boats with gifts of flowers sink on New Year's Eve.

T or F Brazil is the largest producer of Brazil nuts.

Find the answers in this book.

3

Contents

THE **BIG** TRUTH!

In Brazil, soccer is called futebol. It is Brazil's most popular sport.

Carnival is a huge celebration just before Lent. Lent is a period of self-sacrifice and fasting that leads up to Easter.

CHAPTER 1

Welcome to Brazil

It's time for a party! Today is the start of Carnival. This street celebration attracts people from all over the world. Along the parade route, or Sambódromo, community samba schools dance. A year-round effort goes into the performances. Costumes are elaborate. But Brazil is known for much more than its colorful parades.

Early settlers from Portugal brought Carnival to Brazil.

Brazil's Rain Forest

Brazil is the fifth-largest country in the world. It is also the fifth most populated. Brazil has the largest tropical rain forest in the world—the Amazon rain forest. The Amazon contains millions of different kinds of plants and animals. More species live there than anywhere else on the planet. Many species have never been recorded.

Howler monkeys share the rain forest with about 30 million kinds of insects!

Howler monkeys make a loud roaring sound. They can be heard from two miles (3.2 kilometers) away.

People burn parts of the rain forest to clear it. There is little chance for the plants or animals to survive.

Brazil's government works to protect this **unique** area. However, Brazil's population is growing fast. People often chop down parts of the rain forest for timber. They also turn them into farmland. The government must balance its people's needs with the task of preserving the rain forest. This forest is sometimes called the "lungs of the earth." That is because its millions of plants absorb more carbon dioxide and pump out more oxygen than happens anywhere else on our planet.

This monument in Portugal honors famous early Portuguese explorers, such as Pedro Álvares Cabral.

Cabral

CHAPTER 2

The Land of Brazil

On April 22, 1500, a Portuguese explorer spotted land in South America. Pedro Álvares Cabral ordered his fleet of ships to land. He claimed the land for Portugal. He named it Vera Cruz. The land was later renamed Brazil.

Cabral meant to sail to Asia. He drifted off course. He landed in Brazil instead!

PEDRO ÁLVARES CABRAL

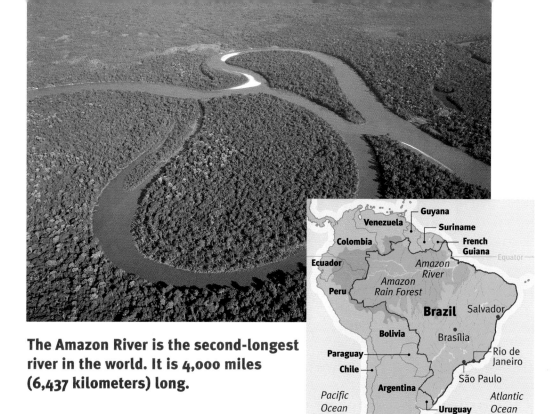

The Amazon River is the second-longest river in the world. It is 4,000 miles (6,437 kilometers) long.

Vast and Varied Landscape

Brazil is the largest country in South America. It shares borders with ten other South American countries. Brazil has rain forests and mountains. It has dry plains and beaches. Brazil's Amazon region covers most of the north. The long Amazon River begins its journey in Peru. It travels east across Brazil to the Atlantic Ocean.

Brazil has many beautiful white-sand beaches on its Atlantic coast.

Summer in January

Most of Brazil lies south of the **equator**. This means that winter begins in July. Summer starts in January. The hottest area of the country is found in the north, along the equator. Temperatures stay at about 80°F (27°C) for most of the year. Brazil's eastern boundary is the Atlantic Ocean.

Living off the Land

Brazil is rich in natural resources. It has large supplies of minerals, timber, and fish. Crops grow well in its warm, wet climate. Brazil is one of the leading **exporters** of coffee and soybeans. It exports more coffee and oranges than any other country.

Brazil's factories produce many different products. Workers make cars, planes, submarines, and steel. They make clothing and shoes. Many of these items are sold to other countries.

The ball-shaped fruits of Brazil-nut trees contain as many as 24 seeds, or nuts.

Brazil exports Brazil nuts. However, Bolivia is the world's leading exporter of Brazil nuts.

Lethal Vines

Lianas, or vines, twist themselves around the trunks of trees in the Amazon rain forest. The lianas also connect the trees. They provide pathways above the ground for monkeys and other animals. One kind of liana, the curare (ku-RAH-ree), has other uses too. Some of Brazil's **indigenous** people carve blowgun darts from the vines. Hunters use these curare-poisoned darts to kill animals. The curare poison stops all muscle activity. The animal stops breathing and dies.

Recently, scientists have found that curare has the power to relax muscles. Doctors use it as an **anesthetic** before surgery. Curare is also used to treat diseases that affect muscles, such as multiple sclerosis and Parkinson's disease.

15

Sub-Canopy

Woody vines climb up the trees in the sub-canopy. They reach toward the light.

Understory

Ferns grow well in the dim light of the understory.

Forest Floor

Termites eat plant litter, such as bark and leaves. They live on the forest floor. They live in large groups.

The Forest Layers

THE **BIG** TRUTH!

The tropical rain forest is home to many kinds of plants and animals. It has four main layers. Trees as tall as 165 feet (50 meters) make up the top layer, called the canopy. The layer below the canopy is called the sub-canopy. Nearly three-quarters of the rain-forest plants and animals live in this layer. Below this layer is the shady understory. Plants in the understory receive very little light. The bottom layer is the forest floor. It is cool, dark, and damp.

Canopy

Epiphytes (EHP-uh-fyts), such as bromeliads, grow on other plants. They thrive in the canopy. Animals come to drink the water that collects in their leaf clusters.

In the Amazon rain forest, many indigenous people live as they have for hundreds of years. However, much of today's native population has become part of mainstream Brazilian social and political life.

CHAPTER 3

Brazil's History

People had lived in Brazil long before Pedro Álvares Cabral "discovered" it in 1500. When the Portuguese sailors arrived, several million indigenous people farmed, fished, and hunted there. These inhabitants lived in small communities. **Archaeologists** estimate that Brazil once had about 1,000 different indigenous groups.

Today, indigenous people make up about one percent of Brazil's population.

Brazil is still one of the world's leading sugarcane producers.

Under Portuguese Rule

In the 1530s, many Portuguese people settled in Brazil. They grew sugarcane on **plantations**. They forced indigenous Brazilians to work for them. Many laborers died from the terrible conditions. Many more died from diseases brought to Brazil by the Europeans.

So many indigenous people died that the Portuguese ran out of workers. They began **enslaving** people from Africa. They transported them to Brazil. The slaves were forced to work on the plantations. The sugar produced brought great wealth to the Portuguese landowners and Portuguese royalty.

In 1888, slavery was ended. About 750,000 slaves were freed.

Brazil and Its Ruling Family

In 1807, France attacked and invaded Portugal. Portugal's ruler was Prince João (zhoh-OW). He escaped to Brazil in 1808. For 13 years, he ran his empire from Brazil. Prince João eventually returned to Portugal. He left his son Pedro behind to run the **colony**. On September 7, 1822, Pedro declared Brazil to be an independent nation. By 1824, Portugal reluctantly agreed with him.

Brazil's Time Line

1808
Rio de Janeiro becomes home to rulers of the Portuguese Empire. It is Brazil's first capital.

1891
Brazil elects its first president, Manoel Deodoro da Fonseca.

The early years of the new nation were **chaotic**. Pedro did not get along with many important Brazilians. After nine years, he handed over power to his five-year-old son Pedro II. He then left Brazil. A series of men tried to hold Brazil together until the boy was old enough to rule the country. In 1840, Pedro II became ruler at age fourteen.

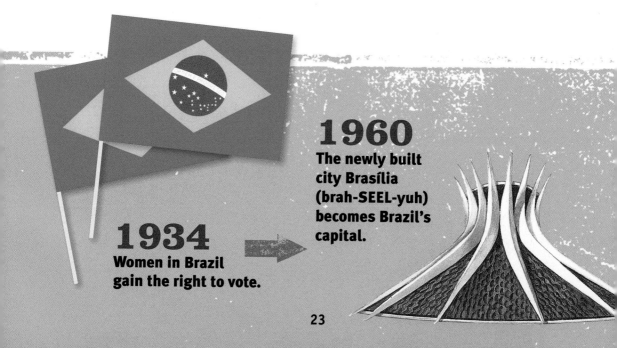

1934
Women in Brazil gain the right to vote.

1960
The newly built city Brasília (brah-SEEL-yuh) becomes Brazil's capital.

Military and Civilian Rule

In 1888, Pedro II ended slavery in Brazil. Many
military leaders and plantation owners were upset
by this. They wanted to rid Brazil of its ruler. In
1889, they led a successful **coup** against Pedro II.
On November 15, 1889, Brazil became a **republic**.

Throughout the 1900s, there were a number
of times that the military took control of the
country. In 1985, military rule in Brazil ended.
Since then, Brazil has had a civilian government.

**In 1985, many people celebrated Brazil's democratic election.
It was the first in more than 20 years.**

Zero Hunger

In 2002, a man born into a poor, working-class family became president of Brazil. Luiz Inácio Lula da Silva was unable to read until he was ten years old. He worked at an early age to help his family. Later, Lula formed the Workers' Party. He fought for workers' rights. He helped Brazil's poor.

Lula's government still works hard to end social problems, such as poverty and hunger. His Fome Zero (Zero Hunger) program provides food coupons and money to about nine million poor families.

The traditional dress
in Salvador is a mix of
African and Portuguese
styles. Salvador is in
northeast Brazil. It was
founded in 1549.

CHAPTER 4

A Blend of Cultures

Salvador was a center for sugar plantations and the slave trade. Its African cultural heritage can still be seen.

Brazil's people are descended from African slaves, Portuguese settlers, and indigenous Brazilians. They are also descended from other **immigrants**. These immigrants have come mostly from Spain, Germany, Italy, and Japan. All these groups have contributed to the country's culture.

Traditional Dance

Brazil's dance styles were influenced by its many cultures. The Frevo can be traced back to Brazil's Portuguese roots. It is performed during Carnival. Frevo dancers carry small umbrellas. They perform high jumps. The umbrellas make the performance look spectacular. They also help the dancers keep their balance.

The Yanomami (yah-nuh-MAH-mee) live in the Brazilian rain forest. They weave baskets from lianas.

Sometimes Yanomami paint themselves with spots and squiggly lines.

Traditional Crafts

Weaving is a tradition among Brazil's indigenous peoples. They weave everyday objects, such as baskets, from palm fronds and grasses. They also make pottery objects. They shape clay into bowls and pots. They dry them in the sun. Then they carve decorative geometric shapes on the objects.

Brazil's Architecture

Traditionally, Brazil's indigenous people built their homes of local materials. They made their homes from wood, grasses, and leaves. Walls built of woven plants allow breezes to cool the interior. When the Portuguese settled in Brazil, they brought European architectural styles with them.

Salvador has many historic buildings. It has large open spaces, called plazas.

The government buildings in Brasília are located along wide streets in the city's center.

Brasília is the country's capital. It shows off the skills of Brazil's modern architects. The city was planned and built in the 1950s. Every detail was thought out, from the number of schools in each neighborhood to the location of all the city's hotels. From above, Brasília resembles an airplane or a bird. The homes are in the "wings." The businesses are in the "nose."

On December 31, many people dress in white. They throw gifts such as flowers into the sea.

CHAPTER 5

Life and Language

It is December 31. Hundreds of people are walking toward the beach with gifts of flowers. It is the annual festival of Iemanjá (eh-man-ZHAH). Iemanjá is the goddess of the sea. Her story can be traced back to African traditions. People put gifts for the goddess in tiny boats. They push the boats out to sea. They pray for Iemanjá's blessing for the next year.

If the boats sink, it means that Iemanjá will grant the people their wishes.

Brazilian Beliefs

The Portuguese converted many people to Roman Catholicism. Today, Brazil has more Catholics than any other country in the world.

Slaves from Africa brought their own religions. However, the Portuguese landowners forced the slaves to practice Catholicism. The slaves blended their own beliefs with Catholicism. They created religions such as Candomblé (kahn-dohm-BLEH).

This huge statue of Jesus overlooks Rio de Janeiro. Rio is Brazil's second-largest city.

The statue took five years to construct.

The Tupí-Guaraní (too-PEE-gwah-rah-NEE) language was spoken in Brazil before the arrival of the Portuguese. It is still spoken today.

Language

Most Brazilians speak Portuguese. However, the pronunciation and some vocabulary differ from what is spoken in Portugal. Brazilian Portuguese includes words from Brazil's many indigenous languages. Today, most indigenous people speak Portuguese as well as their native language.

Soccer, Soccer, Soccer

Soccer is the most popular sport in Brazil. Every four years, sports fans in Brazil and around the world get soccer fever. The World Cup is probably the world's most popular sports contest. The Brazilian team has won it five times.

The Brazilian people are not just fans of soccer, they're fanatics! The greatest soccer player of all time, Pelé (peh-LEH), is Brazilian. He was only seventeen when he played in his first World Cup. He was in Brazil's soccer team when it won the World Cup in 1958, 1962, and 1970.

Brazil is the only country to have played in every World Cup contest.

Favelas are sometimes perched on steep hillsides. Homes in favelas are often built by the families themselves.

CHAPTER 6

Living in Brazil

Brazil is a large country with many people. A small number of Brazilians have great wealth. Some families live in houses in the suburbs. In cities, middle-class families live in apartments in large high-rise buildings. Poor families who live in cities usually live in crowded settlements. These are called favelas.

About four-fifths of Brazil's people live in cities.

It's Time for School

Education is free in Brazil. All children aged
between seven and fourteen must go to school.
Some children attend private schools. However,
it can be difficult to ensure that everyone in Brazil
attends school. Many children come from poor
families. They must leave school early
in order to earn money for their family.
Many children leave as soon as
they are fourteen.

Perfect Goal

The Gol de Letra ("Perfect Goal") Foundation is a nonprofit organization. It was set up in 1998 by former Brazilian football stars Raí (left) and Leonardo (right). Its aim is to help children living in the poorest favelas of Rio, São Paulo, and Niterói. Some of the children have never attended school. The organization hopes to contribute to the children's educational and cultural development. It offers them the chance to take part in dance, music, art, literature, computer, or sports activities.

Family, Food, and Fun!

Whether Brazilians live in large cities or small villages, they often stay close to their extended family. Many families enjoy a Sunday meal together. The national dish of Brazil is *feijoada* (fay-zho-AH-da). This is a stew of beef, pork, and black beans. It is served with collard greens, oranges, and rice.

Brazilians know how to enjoy themselves. Brazil's green parks and white-sand beaches are always full of people celebrating life in their sunny homeland! ★

True Statistics

Official name: Federative Republic of Brazil

Size: 3,300,171 square miles (8,547,403 square kilometers)

Population: About 190 million

Official language: Portuguese

Largest city in Brazil: São Paulo

Population of São Paulo: More than 17 million

Largest soccer stadium: Maracanã Stadium, Rio

Catholics in Brazil: About 75 percent of the population

Number of rivers in Brazil: More than 1,000

Internet country code: br

Internet users: About 43 million

Did you find the truth?

(T) It is a lucky sign if boats with gifts of flowers sink on New Year's Day.

(F) Brazil is the largest producer of Brazil nuts.

Resources

Books

Albert, Toni. *The Remarkable Rainforest:
An Active-Learning Book for Kids*.
Mechanicsburg, PA: Trickle Creek Books, 2003.

Behnke, Alison and Duro, Karin L. *Cooking
the Brazilian Way*. Minneapolis: Lerner
Publishing Group, 2004.

Castaldo, Nancy F. *Rainforests: An Activity Guide
for Ages 6–9*. Chicago: Chicago Review Press,
2003.

Cherry, Lynne. *The Great Kapok Tree: A Tale of
the Amazon Rain Forest*. New York: Voyager
Books, 2000.

Fontes, Justine and Ron. *Brazil* (A to Z Series).
New York: Children's Press, 2003.

Fowler, Allan. *South America*. New York:
Children's Press, 2001.

Hollander, Malika. *Brazil: The Culture*.
New York: Crabtree Publishing Company, 2003.

Streissguth, Thomas. *Brazil in Pictures*.
Minneapolis: Lerner Publishing
Group, 2003.

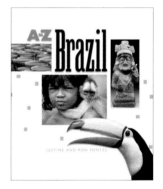

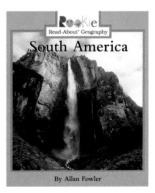

Organizations and Web Sites

TIME for Kids: Brazil
www.timeforkids.com/TFK/hh/goplaces/main/
0,20344,635502,00.html
Explore a kid's-eye view of Brazil and learn some Portuguese.

The Brazilian Embassy in Washington, D.C.
www.brasilemb.org/cultural/school_project.shtml
This Web site has plenty of links to information about Brazil.

Arbor Day Foundation
www.arborday.org/programs/rainforest/kids.cfm
Explore rain forests in Brazil and around the world and learn about what you can do to help them.

Places to Visit

Iguaçu National Park
Rodovia BR 469, KM 18
Foz do Iguaçu
Paraná, Brazil
+55 (45) 3521-4400
www.cataratasdoiguacu.com.
br/index_en.asp
Visit the amazing falls on the border of Brazil and Argentina and view some local wildlife.

National Historical Museum
Praça Marechal Âncora
Próximo à Praça XV
Rio de Janeiro, Brazil
+55 (21) 240-2092
www.museuhistoriconacional.
com.br/ingles
Learn about the rich history of Brazil and view ancient artifacts.

Important Words

anesthetic (an-iss-THET-ik) – a drug given to people to prevent them from feeling pain

archaeologist (ar-kee-OL-uh-jist) – a scientist who learns about people of the past by studying ancient objects

chaotic (kay-OT-ik) – totally confusing

colony (KOL-uh-nee) – a settlement under the rule of a parent country

coup (KOO) – the sudden, and often violent, overthrow of a government

enslave – to make someone a slave

equator (i-KWAY-tur) – an imaginary line around the middle of the earth, halfway between the North and South poles

export – to sell goods to another country

immigrant (IM-uh-gruhnt) – a person who arrives from one country to live in another

indigenous (in-DIJ-uh-nuhss) – the original people living in an area

plantation – a large farm on which, usually, only one crop is grown

republic – a type of government in which laws are made by a group of people elected by the country's citizens

unique (yoo-NEEK) – unlike anything else; one of a kind

Index

About the Author

Tara Walters enjoys traveling to other countries and learning about their history, people, and culture. She loves history and geography so much that she studied it at the University of Notre Dame. She is a first-generation Irish American who spends part of each year in Ireland. Tara lives in New Jersey, with her sons, husband, and two dogs.

PHOTOGRAPHS: Big Stock Photo (Alex Bramwell, p. 13; Elder Salles, p. 22; David Davis, p. 38; Stephen Rees, p. 3 and p. 14); Digital Vision (p. 9); Getty Images (cover; p. 6; p. 25; p. 29; p. 31; p. 36); iStockPhoto.com (Flamming Mahler, p. 20; Franck Camhi, p. 34); Photolibrary (p. 26; p. 28; p. 40); © The Granger Collection, New York (p. 21); Tranz/Corbis (pp. 10–13; p. 15; p. 18; p. 24; p. 30; p. 32; p. 35; pp. 41–42). All other images property of Weldon Owen Education.